MOTIVATION
IS
P.E.A.R.
SHAPED

MOTIVATION IS P.E.A.R. SHAPED

SIMON HARTLEY

First published in Great Britain in 2024 by Be World Class.

Copyright © Simon Hartley 2024

The moral right of the author has been asserted.

A CIP catalogue record of this book is available from the British Library.

ISBN 978-1-3999-7920-7

Typeset in EB Garamond by Louise Carrier.

Printed and bound in Great Britain.

Be World Class Ltd

Lister House

Lister Hill

Leeds

LS18 5DZ

be-world-class.com

ACKNOWLEDGMENTS

"No one succeeds alone. No one."
Gary Keller, American entrepreneur.

I could not have written this book without the help
and support of a few fantastic people.

Firstly, my wonderful wife and daughters who
support me in everything I do.

I'd also like to say a huge thank you to Rich Jones for writing the
Foreword, and for absolutely embracing P.E.A.R.-shaped motivation.

And, last but by no means least, the amazing Louise Carrier for her
brilliant cover design, illustrations, typesetting and publication support.

PREFACE

"Preach what you practice.
Don't practice what you preach."

These are the sage words of wisdom a friend of mine shared a few years ago. As soon as he said it, I started to see the subtle but profound distinction between preaching what you practice and practicing what you preach.

Those who adopt the 'practice what you preach' philosophy are often trying desperately to do the things they tell others. Over the years I've come across hundreds of coaches who are trying (and often struggling) to do the things they tell their clients. I've seen 'mindset coaches' who fall into the same traps they attempt to help others avoid. I've seen fitness professionals and personal trainers trying to discipline themselves so that they stick to their own exercise and diet plan. It's often a long-term struggle to take their own advice.

Preaching what you practice is different.

When we preach what we practice, we simply share those things that we already do on a daily basis. Often, we're sharing the methods and approaches that work for us. These tend to be the tried and tested methods that have made our lives easier and helped us achieve a degree of success. Sometimes these approaches have been transformational. They've created a paradigm shift of some kind and radically changed our perspective. We could describe them as 'game changers'. And when we share these approaches with others, we see the impact it has for them too.

This is what my understanding of P.E.A.R.-shaped motivation has done for me.

And that is why I'm sharing it with you now.

FOREWORD

---

by Rich Jones,
former British elite triathlon champion turned Training Manager at Abbott Nutrition.

Motivation is vital in the highly pressurised world of a sales team.

It's easy when things are going well, but tough to sustain if things are going badly, especially when it's no fault of your own.

Simon has helped the team understand the importance of developing four strong pillars of motivation; a vital ingredient to developing a high-performance team.

Momentum is everything. Leadership is key. Understanding what motivates our team has been a major step in moving the needle.

The P.E.A.R. method has been adopted and implemented by the leadership and training team to ensure each member fulfils their potential and always maintains strong motivation.

It is the missing ingredient to sustaining motivation in all facets of your life.

CONTENTS

INTRODUCTION

Motivation...

We know how important it is.

We understand how it impacts on our performance and success. We've felt the powerful drive when we have it. It can feel like we have afterburners on full thrust. And we probably know how tough it is to achieve anything if we don't.

Of course, in a team environment, it's not just our own motivation that we need to consider. I continually hear leaders asking how they can motivate their people. In fact, I've been asked questions like...

"How can you motivate the unmotivated?"

Unsurprisingly, there are a few 'usual suspect' myths that I see doing the rounds, such as...

"You can't motivate others. People can only motivate themselves."

"You're either a motivated person or an unmotivated person. Motivation is a personality trait."

"Everyone has their price. You just need the right incentive."

"If you want to motivate someone, just praise them."

"Fear is the ultimate motivator."

"Human beings are motivated to move toward pleasure and avoid pain."

"If you're struggling to motivate someone, you either need a bigger carrot or a bigger stick."

I suspect you've come across a few of these yourself. In fact, you may be looking at one or two of them and thinking, "Is that really a myth?" For example, you might be thinking that we humans are motivated to go toward pleasure and avoid pain. Many of us are on a lot of occasions. But there are notable exceptions. Arguably, those who run into burning buildings to rescue others, or those who opt to go to war, are not going toward pleasure and avoiding pain.

I suspect we buy into some of these because we're looking for a nice, tidy, simple explanation. However, the problem is that many of the explanations we've been given are built on unstable foundations.

So often, these 'rules' of motivation fall down because they don't work for everyone all the time.

When we reflect on our own life experience, we tend to see that motivation is personal.

What works for one person, doesn't necessarily work for another. We might also see that the context or situation has a huge impact on motivation. What drives us in one situation may not motivate us in another.

———————

So, knowing the complexities...

How can we motivate ourselves?

How can we motivate others?

Motivation starts with a Y

I often say that motivation starts with a Y. Then, of course I qualify this. Alphabetically, motivation starts with an 'M'. But psychologically, it starts with a 'why?' — the question 'why?', not the letter 'Y'. In fact, motivation is often described in psychology as 'the why of behaviour.' Understanding motivation often requires us to understand the reason we do things... or don't do things.

Sharing this understanding with business leaders then sparks a question...

'Why do your people come to work?'

The headline answer of course tends to be, "Because they need money... to feed themselves, feed their families, keep a roof over their heads, etc."

That could be the reason they work. But why do they work here? Why do they do this job, in this organisation?

I ask a refined version of this question to employees. I ask, **"Why do you come here and do this job, with us?"**

In fact, I've asked this question thousands of times during the last few decades, in all kinds of organisations — large and small — spanning a wide variety of industries and sectors, including business, education, healthcare, elite sport, charities, and the military. I've also asked this question to the most senior people (CEOs, MDs, etc.), right down to the most junior who are often on minimum wage.

As you might imagine, there are many different answers. Interestingly though, they all fall into four distinct categories. That's why I say that motivation is P.E.A.R.-shaped.

P.E.A.R. is an acronym.

P STANDS FOR 'PURPOSE'

Some people are motivated because they understand the intrinsic value of what they do. They know that they are making a difference and having a positive impact. In many cases they know that they are contributing to something that has genuine importance. Many people are motivated by the knowledge that what they do changes lives for the better or has a positive impact on the world.

_____

E STANDS FOR 'ENJOYMENT'

Many people are motivated because they enjoy what they do. This enjoyment can come because the task is fun. Often people enjoy what they feel they're good at. On many occasions, people enjoy the challenge and the mental stimulation of pushing themselves. Others may enjoy working with a great team, or with great customers. There are a variety of ways to gain enjoyment from work.

_____

A STANDS FOR 'ACHIEVEMENT'
(and also Ambition)

It won't surprise you to know that this motivates many athletes. Many athletes work for years to win a gold medal. But, as a friend of mine once said, "The medal is just a metal disc on a ribbon." To understand what's really motivating these athletes, we need to know what winning the medal means. Perhaps it's because the gold medal means they are 'the best'. For others, the real motivation is to achieve their potential or know that they're improving and developing. Either way, they are motivated by 'achievement'.

_____

R STANDS FOR 'REWARD' (and Recognition)

This can come in the form of money, but money is not the only form of reward. For many people, what they do becomes rewarding when they get recognition. This might be formal, for example receiving an award. Equally, it might come in the form of positive feedback and recognition that they've done a great job.

In my experience, we are all motivated by all of these factors, but in different proportions. Some people are heavily driven by rewards. Others are primarily purpose-driven. It helps to know what is driving us personally, because it allows us to start mastering our own motivation. Experience also tells me that if we're over-reliant on one of these elements, we could find that our motivation is vulnerable. For example, if we're highly driven by rewards and making money, we will really struggle if the cash dries up.

I often see these four categories as 'pillars' of motivation. It therefore makes sense to have four strong pillars. If our motivation is too 'one dimensional' (i.e., too dependent on one pillar), it tends to be unstable and vulnerable.

This all goes to show that motivation is a pretty complex concept. It's not simply a case of waving cash in front of an individual or putting a gun to their heads to get more effort from them. It helps us realise that people aren't either 'highly motivated' or 'completely unmotivated' and that motivation is something we can influence and master.

PURPOSE

ENJOYMENT

ACHIEVEMENT AND ALSO AMBITION

REWARD AND RECOGNITION

CHAPTER 1

P is for Purpose

"He who has a why to live can bear any how."
Viktor Frankl, 1959

Viktor Frankl was a Jewish psychiatrist, living in Vienna at the outbreak of World War II. As you can imagine, Austria was not a great place to be at a time when Nazi Germany was gaining power in Europe. Because Frankl was a respected academic, several universities in the United States offered him the opportunity to escape Europe and take up residence there. He turned them down, choosing instead to stay with his family. Soon afterwards, he and his family were captured by the Nazis. They were separated and taken into concentration camps. Not long after being sent to Theresienstadt, Viktor Frankl learned that his father had died at the hands of the Nazis. During the next two years he also lost his mother and new wife. He endured years of suffering as he moved from camp to camp. In his book, *Man's Search for Meaning*, Viktor Frankl describes both the incredible adversity that he and the other prisoners experienced, and also how they coped. He noticed that those with a strong reason to live often survived. However, if their will to live faded, they quickly followed.

I've noticed that a strong 'why' is critical, especially if we want to achieve something extraordinary or we're taking on tough challenges.

When I wrote *How to Shine*, I studied a dozen world-class individuals, such as a Michelin-starred chef, a world-record-breaking polar explorer, a leading mountaineer, successful athletes and even a world-champion barista.

Unsurprisingly, people like this tend to have enormous goals. They are the kind of people that want to win Olympic gold medals, break world records, and win world championships.

What may surprise you is that this ambition does not distinguish top performers. I've met hundreds of young athletes who all want to become the world champion. I've stood in front of squads of teenage athletes and said, "Hands up if you want to win Olympic gold or be crowned world champion." Of course, all the hands go up. And yet, not all of them reach their goal.

The truth is... lots of people want to win the gold medal. But some people want it more than others.

As well as studying world-class performers, I've also studied those who have taken on enormous challenges. When I wrote *Could I Do That?*, I studied a handful of people that had all achieved 'the impossible', to find out how. But learning from others only gives me part of the picture. Sometimes I need to experience things for myself, to truly understand them. So, over the years, I've taken on a few rather daft challenges myself — some physical, some intellectual. This helps me appreciate what goes on between our ears — how we think and feel — when we hit the really tough moments.

My experience of working with and studying extreme high-performers tells me that they're tenacious. In simple terms, they don't give up. No matter how tough it gets, they keep going. I also knew that it's a characteristic that I didn't have in great abundance. I couldn't honestly say I'd ever pushed myself to my limits. In fact, if I was truly honest, I'd say I often threw in the towel when things got uncomfortable. So, I created one particularly mad challenge to learn how to push past 'the quit point'.

The challenge was to walk 100 miles in 24 hours. It's not something most of us can just wake up one day and do. My preparation spanned 15 months. I started by increasing my average walking speed to five miles per hour, then I increased the duration and distance. Training taught me a few key lessons, such as the importance of having the right footwear and how to rehydrate and refuel on the move. It also helped build my fitness and stamina.

With the training behind me, I set off one summer's evening at 9pm. I had planned a route, constructed of eight 12.5-mile laps, that started and finished at my house. This meant I could refill my backpack with food and drink, go to the toilet and so on, without the need for a 'road crew' or support vehicle.

At the half-way point, about 7.30am the following morning, I stopped briefly to replenish my supplies and change my socks. My mistake was to sit down. As I stood up and started walking again, my body seized up. Within a few hundred metres I had excruciating pain in both legs — it felt like both knees were being stabbed by a spear. Every step was agony, and I knew my comfy sofa was less than a mile away.

I hobbled down the road for a mile or so with a battle raging in my head.

"Why are you doing this?"

"Are you some kind of sadomasochist?"

"Why don't you just quit?"

"No-one is watching. You've done well to get this far."

And then it hit me.

When you're faced with a quit point, there are two questions you need to answer.

1. Why am I doing this?

2. How much do I want it?

If you can answer these well, you're likely to get through. If not, you'll probably quit. It brings us right back to the importance of our 'why'.

Often this 'why' comes from a strong sense of purpose.

The power of 'why'

Simon Sinek (2009) emphasises this element in his book, *Start With Why*. He says, **"People don't buy what you do. They buy why you do it."** He's not just talking about why customers buy certain products. He also argues that this thinking explains why we give our votes to certain politicians and why some employees give blood, sweat and tears to their employer. In his TEDx Talk, he shares a few examples, such as the Wright Brothers, who achieved the first powered flight. Logically, you might have expected their biggest rival, Samuel Pierpoint Langley, to reach this milestone first. It was Langley who had the backing of the War Department, $50,000 in funding and a team of experts from Harvard and the Smithsonian Institution behind him. In comparison, the Wright Brothers funded their endeavours using the profits from their bicycle shop. Simon Sinek explains that the Wright Brothers and their support team were powered by the cause — their belief that powered flight could change the world — whereas Langley was motivated by the prospect of fame and riches. Sinek also argues that Apple have access to the same technology, marketplace, and talent as most computer companies. And yet, Apple are renowned as the great innovators and have developed an almost cult-like following of loyal customers. The reason, in Simon Sinek's view, is that they share their purpose and beliefs, not just the features and benefits of their products.

As he explains it, people don't engage with your 'what' or 'how', they engage with your 'why'. It reflects the understanding that much of our human behaviour and decision-making is driven by the emotional areas of our brain, not the logical and rational parts.

When I hear athletes say, "I want to win the gold medal," my response is often to ask, "Why?" I remember having this conversation with an Olympic swimmer, who I worked with for around eight years. I suspect it surprised him when, one day, I asked...

"So why do you do this? Why do you get up at daft o'clock in the morning, drive to the pool, plough up and down in chlorinated water for two hours, see the physio, lift weights, have a spot of lunch, see me, then drive back to the pool to charge up and down for another couple of hours? You do this day-after-day, week-after-week, for years. It's ridiculous if you think about it. What's it all for?"

His immediate response was to say, "It's to get a gold medal."

So, I replied, "Okay. I'm going to pop down to the trophy shop and buy you a medal. Then we can forget all this nonsense."

"No," he said, "that's not it."

And then we started talking about the real 'why'. We started talking about what a gold medal meant. Interestingly, he started by saying, "the gold medal means I'm the best," before realising that being the best didn't really matter to him. After a little more thought, he concluded that his reason to swim was to explore his potential, push himself and become the best he could be. In this period of his life, he was exploring his potential through swimming. When he retired from swimming, he'd simply transfer this to another field. Having retired from competitive swimming in 2008, he now explores his potential through speaking, mentoring, and leading his swim school business. Interestingly, he also realised that his true goal was not to win the gold medal, but to retire saying, "No regrets."

I've had a similar conversation with a team I'm currently working with. They are competing in the next Olympic Games. They are also aiming for gold. Their nation expects it. In fact, there is an accepted understanding that a silver medal equals failure. But, whilst the gold medal might be our goal and target, it needs to have meaning. There has to be a solid reason.

Whilst I was in Fiji with them, I asked the question. What does winning an Olympic gold medal mean to you... your teammates... your families and communities... and the nation? We talked about the amount of dedication required, the workload, the training and the 'sacrifices' (choices), they'll need to make if they're going to genuinely compete for gold.

Everyone says they want to win.
Some want it more than others.

What will you do that your opponents won't do?

Why are you doing it?

Who are you doing it for?

Experience tells me that simply avoiding failure is not the healthiest reason. History is littered with examples of athletes, such as Tiger Woods, Victoria Pendleton, and Jonny Wilkinson, who were driven by obsession or fear of failure and became incredibly successful. I've noticed that, if obsession and fear of failure are the drivers, success is likely to be accompanied by misery. There are other athletes, such as Marat Safin, the Russian tennis player who was motivated to escape poverty. Interestingly, Marat Safin's form declined drastically after he'd won his Grand Slam titles and made his first few millions. There's no doubt that simply having a powerful reason, however unhealthy, can get you a long way. But I would argue that those who are driven by passion and curiosity tend to sustain their success. Their motivation tends to be more stable and enduring.

That's okay for athletes. How does this apply to business?

Understanding our purpose is also important in business. Some organisations have an obvious purpose, which people buy into. In some cases, their purpose is to save lives. I remember delivering a session at the Royal National Lifeboat Institute (RNLI) head office a few years ago. They are very clear about their purpose. Importantly, their people not only understand the purpose of the organisation, but they also feel it. They understand their own personal connection to it and how they contribute to it. This doesn't just apply to those who jump into lifeboats and rescue people at sea. It applies equally to those who work in the gift shop, the accounts team, IT or human resources.

Of course, not all organisations save lives. So, how does this principle apply to those working in a bank, for example?

Most businesses have targets and goals. Interestingly, most of the goals I've seen are financial. Most of them are numbers that end in a zero. And the vast majority of goals that I've seen mean very little to the people who are tasked to deliver them.

In January 2019, I was asked to help the senior leadership team in a UK high-street bank with a 'goal-setting' exercise for their people. The senior leaders had been reviewing their strategy and identified an opportunity. One of their income streams typically delivered around £4 million per year in revenue. The senior leadership team had looked at the opportunity in the market and felt there was potential to earn £40 million per year.

Their challenge... to raise the team's annual target by a factor of ten.

The problem was, their team were used to targets that rose by 10–15% per year, not by 1000%.

How could they engage their people on this 'ridiculous' target?

We got the team together in Birmingham for the day. Before even discussing the target, I asked them, **"Why do you do what you do? Why is it important? Why does it matter? How does it make a difference?"**

The team told me that, as a bank, they lend money. I asked what that money was used for. They said, "It helps build schools and hospitals, to repair roads and railways, etc." We all agreed that lending this money had a positive impact on society. So, I said, "Imagine if we could do more of that. Imagine if we could do twice as much... five times as much... ten times as much. What if we could help build ten times as many schools and hospitals, or repair ten times as many roads. How much impact would that have?"

When we understand this, our goal or target has meaning. It takes on an importance. It becomes more than just some ludicrous number that an executive in an office dreamt up. It goes beyond any personal, ego-driven, ambition. And therefore, it becomes engaging.

In my view, this is the power of purpose.

However...

Experience also tells me that purpose alone is not enough. Whilst I appreciate where Simon Sinek is coming from, I've also learned there are more dimensions to motivation. I've chatted with business leaders who say, very legitimately, "That's fine for some organisations, but many of my people are just here to earn a wage. Quite frankly, they don't give a stuff about some grand purpose. They're just here to get paid."

So, if we want to understand motivation, we need to look beyond purpose.

CHAPTER 2

E is for enjoyment

"Do what you love and love what you do."

Those are the final words that I wrote in *How to Shine*. It's the way I summarised what I'd learned about top performers. On one level, it's an incredibly sound principle that sets the foundation for world-class performance. But there's an important context. The people I worked with and studied were all powered by passion. Their love for their field enabled them to achieve success and sustain it. It fuelled their curiosity, which propelled them along a journey of discovery and grew their expertise.

I remember one of the athletes saying, "You need to fall in love with the processes." World-leading mountaineer, Alan Hinkes, talked about his love for "being in the hills." Unlike many other climbers, he wasn't overly fixated on reaching the summit. He was able to focus on the journey. It meant that he often decided to wait for an ideal weather window, and took a little longer, before attempting the final push. In his experience, many mountaineers die because they go too early in their desperation to reach the top. As Alan explained, "Getting home is the goal. The summit is a bonus."

This philosophy also enables elite performers to try things and fail, because they're not purely driven by the need for success. This kind of mindset enables them to 'push the envelope' as I describe it, to challenge themselves and step way outside of their comfort zone. Of course, this is a critical ingredient for anyone that wants to excel.

I consider myself to be very fortunate. I love what I do. I follow my curiosity and passion. It's almost the embodiment of Mark Twain's quote (which may have originated from Confucius or Marc Anthony) and has been shared by many others since:

> **"Find a job you enjoy doing and you'll never have to work a day in your life."**

Over the years, I've seen this kind of advice regurgitated time after time in the self-improvement and personal development world.

"Follow your passion."

"Do what you love and then find a way to make it pay."

... and so on.

I deliberately say, "It's *almost* the embodiment." I'll be perfectly honest. Whilst I enjoy many of the tasks, it's still work. It feels like work. Sometimes, it's particularly hard work. There are lots of less interesting bits, like writing reports and going through the accounts. It's definitely not all sunshine and roses. So, whilst the sentiment sounds great, I'm not entirely sure it's always realistic. In fact, even for someone like me, you'd call it 'idealistic.'

I'm also acutely aware that not everyone is in the position to do what they love.

There is another side to my quote at the start of this chapter. As well as doing what we love, there's a strong case for learning to love what we do. This also comes with a caveat. I don't imagine for one minute that everyone can become super passionate or develop a deep love for their job. I've spoken to leaders who ask, "What about the cleaners? What about those waiting tables? What about the labourers on the building sites... or people that work down the sewers? Are you saying they can love what they do?"

It's a valid question.

Sometimes the task isn't fun. So, we need to understand 'enjoyment' in a broader context.

"If it's easy, it's boring!"

This is a sentiment I continually hear from people who are at the top of their game. Sometimes they are technical people, such as engineers. It's also true of elite athletes and sports players. I remember mountaineer, Alan Hinkes, explaining why he's drawn to climb K2 or the north face of the Eiger. Neither of them is as high as Everest but, in his view, they are more of a challenge. And that's what makes them interesting.

Mihaly Csikszentmihalyi is a psychologist and researcher who identified and named the psychological state of 'flow'. 'Flow' (which is often referred to as being in 'the zone') is a state of optimal performance and peak experience. Moments of 'flow' are often described as that magical space where everything seems easy or when you feel like you have the Midas touch. It is a state of complete concentration and total absorption. People often report that peak performances seem effortless. They seem to have more time, see things more clearly and find the task easy. It often results in exceptional performance too.

This is Bob Beamon's account of his world-record-breaking long jump.

"There is no answer for the performance. But everything was just perfect for it, the runway, my takeoff — I went six feet in the air when usually I'd go about five — and my concentration was perfect. It never happened quite that way before. I blocked out everything in the world, except my focus on the jump." (Berkow – 1984)

But how do we get into this 'magical' state?

Although we tend to read about examples such as an athlete breaking a world record, we all have the potential to experience peak performances. During your life, you will have experienced moments where you've been 'in the zone'. You may have been writing something, cooking, negotiating a deal, doing a presentation, or building something. The task is irrelevant. Even some apparently mundane tasks can provide people with peak experiences. Mihaly Csikszentmihalyi (2008) gives an example of a man whose job it is to slice fish. Slicing fish may not seem like a particularly engaging task. However, he dedicates his professional life to slicing his fish perfectly. He constantly pushes himself to perfect his technique, so that every slice consistently follows the striations on the flesh. The chef sees his job as an art form, like that of a sculptor.

I have used this same principle when working with a café/restaurant chain. Most people waiting tables or serving food in a busy café wouldn't necessarily focus on achieving a peak performance. Many of the roles would probably be viewed as unskilled or menial. Most waiting staff probably start their shift with the primary aim of getting through it and going home as quickly as possible. However, we sought to adopt a different tack.

As the song says...

"It's not what you do, it's the way that you do it."

I discovered that there are a lot of skilled roles in a café. Making coffee is a prime example. There are around a dozen steps to making a perfect espresso shot, all of which must be executed exceptionally well to produce a great coffee. In addition, for a latte, flat white, or cappuccino, there is a great deal of skill required to get the milk to the optimal consistency and texture. No wonder there is a world championship for baristas.

In that café, our job was not just to make coffee. Our job was to make truly great coffee, and to take pride in the quality of coffee that we produced. We had internal competitions for our baristas and sent them on training courses so that we could make ever better coffee. The same was true of baking bread, preparing smoothies and juices, serving customers, cooking, presenting food and even wiping down tables. How many tables have you seen in restaurants that aren't quite clean? How many servers have you seen wiping crumbs onto the floor or onto a chair? It seems like a very simple task and yet few people manage to execute it consistently well in the middle of a manic Saturday lunchtime shift. As with most things, it is easy to do the job poorly. It's both more challenging, and more rewarding, when we do the job really well.

Q. Why do you like working here?

A. It's the people.

When I ask employees what makes their job enjoyable, many reply, "It's the people." They talk about their team, the people they work with, and the culture. They may not use the word 'culture', but they'll talk about the social and psychological environment and, in particular, how it makes them feel. When they go a little further, I also tend to hear people talk about a sense of camaraderie and togetherness that comes from working in a good team

Interestingly, I've found that having a sense of purpose often provides the catalyst for great teamwork. When I wrote *Stronger Together*, I found that the foundation of great teamwork was a strong, clear, shared purpose. However, it's not the only ingredient.

Over the years I've asked dozens of world-class leaders how they've built great teams. Often their first answer is... "You need great team players."

Fundamentally, you need good people. This is why leading organisations recruit on character — not purely on skills, qualifications, or experience. In his book, *Legacy*, my friend James Kerr (2013) explains the All Blacks' view that,

"culture is collective character."

Essentially, our culture stems from the character of the people within it. Therefore, to get the culture right, we need to recruit people with the right character. James Kerr also shares the simple 'no dickheads' rule that the All Blacks use to protect their culture.

Tom Hill (2010) revolutionised the culture within his family's manufacturing business when they realised the importance of hiring people with the right character and developing character in their existing team. When he took over the business from his father-in-law, the business was struggling. Their once-great company had become a victim of its own success. Being based in a small town, the company started by employing people that the leaders knew personally. One of the benefits of a small town is that everyone knows everyone. If you were a pain-in-the-butt at school, everyone would know. So, in the early days, the business was able to recruit really good people and built a fantastic culture.

The business grew rapidly and needed to hire more people. Gradually the dynamics shifted. They became less picky as they became more desperate for people to fill roles. Instead of hiring good humans that they knew, they began to recruit anyone who could fill a role.

"Can you breathe?... Yes?... Great!... When can you start?"

Of course, this had a profound impact on the culture of the company. Introducing the wrong kind of people quickly diluted the culture they had prided themselves on.

Tom Hill noticed that the character of their people had a dramatic effect on almost every area of the business, so he instigated a change. When they focused on recruiting and selecting those with 'the right character', and developing character in their people, their performance transformed. People became more motivated, productive, and creative. Their rates of absenteeism, health and safety incidents and disciplinary issues plummeted. The enormous rule book they had created, became almost redundant. Managers spent more time solving operational challenges, such as how to improve working practices, and less on 'people issues.'

As Tom Hill emphasises, a business is founded on people. Those with solid character tend to make good decisions because they want to do the right thing. Of course, the by-product is that good performance and results then follow.

And, crucially, it became a more enjoyable place to be.

In my experience, this thinking does not only apply to hiring employees. It is equally applicable to ensuring we select the right client, suppliers, and partners. Many years ago, as I finished a very challenging year working with my first Premier League football club, I committed to a mantra.

Choose your clients carefully!

It's something I am still conscious of today and it determines who I work with. It comes from a very simple principle. I want to wake up each day and look forward to my day. A huge part of that revolves around the people I'll be working with. Therefore, I choose to work with good humans who share similar values. Over the years I've found that this not only leads to enjoyable work, but also successful outcomes.

I've seen the impact that this philosophy has when building communities and delivering events. During the past few years, I've built two communities with friends. One, called *The Curious Mindset*, is a community for technology leaders and is dedicated to helping them develop their leadership skills. The second, called *Success Unlocked*, is for entrepreneurs (often solo entrepreneurs) who are expert practitioners and want to develop their business mindset. We deliver online and in-person events with both communities. It's an absolute pleasure working with both. The people in those communities are genuinely fantastic. We always have a great room of people, which means that I look forward to every session I do with them, and they look forward to being in each other's company.

Of course, this hasn't happened by chance. Both communities are amazing places because the two leaders, Bandish Nayee and Dino Tartaglia, are very selective. They act as gatekeepers. They know that introducing people with the wrong motives and intentions will dilute the culture. They know how to spot the 'good humans', through their choices and behaviours. And they only welcome people who will add to the culture and environment. That's what makes it enjoyable.

But...

As we've discovered, not everyone is motivated by enjoyment. Even those who enjoy what they do tend to need other drivers. Fun is great. But fun alone, without any sense of purpose, can become vacuous and empty. Some would say that enjoyment without a sense of achievement will quickly start to lose its shine. And many would say that an enjoyable workplace is fine, but if it doesn't pay the bills, they'll be looking elsewhere.

So, whilst enjoyment is important, we need to look beyond it to build stable and enduring motivation.

CHAPTER 3

A is for Achievement (and Ambition)

Achievement Motivation is a recognised phenomenon within psychology. The simple premise is that people are motivated by the prospect of achievement and the desire to achieve.

If we step back a little, we'll remember that motivation is often referred to as the 'why of behaviour.' It helps answer questions like, "why do we do the things we do?" That question becomes quite interesting when you look at some of the bizarre things that some humans choose to do.

For example...

Why would anyone dedicate a significant portion of their life to getting a small white ball into a hole in the ground, by hitting it with an odd-shaped club? On the face of it, this seems like a ridiculous activity, particularly when they retrieve the ball almost as soon as it lands in the hole. Why would people spend money on this? Why would they do it in the wind and rain? It's ridiculous!

So, why do millions of people choose to play golf?

One explanation is that they are motivated by a desire to display mastery because a sense of mastery feels good.

Some simple principles from elite sport psychology...

In *Peak Performance Every Time*, I share some simple principles from elite sport psychology. I describe how our mental game works in spirals. There is a positive spiral and a negative spiral. I often draw them out as a model to show how the components, particularly focus, confidence, and motivation, are interdependent. It explains how they underpin and feed each other. It also demonstrates how each spiral is self-perpetuating and compounds.

At this point, I could throw a load of research and theory at you to justify the model. But I'm not going to. There's another form of evidence that is potentially far more powerful.

Your own experience.

Take a look at the positive spiral.

Can you see this reflected in your own life experience?

The Postive Spiral

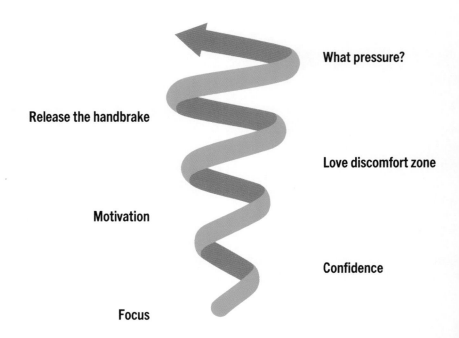

Taken from *Peak Performance Every Time* (Hartley, 2022b).

As you'll see, the base of the spiral has three key ingredients — focus, confidence, and motivation. The foundation of the whole thing is focus. More specifically, we start to build the spiral when we're focused on the right thing at the right time.

When we have a simple, clear job, we have a very good chance of doing that job well. Obviously, we need to have the knowledge, skills, resources, and desire to do it as well. But having a simple, clear task initially gives us a massive advantage.

When we do the job well, we normally get a sense of belief, satisfaction, and fulfilment. Typically, as human beings, we like exhibiting mastery, and we like to be successful in the things we do. So, when we perform well at something, we tend to want to do it again. Psychologists, such as Albert Bandura (1997) have identified strong links between mastery, confidence, achievement, and motivation.

These links set up our positive spiral.

- **When I focus on a simple, clear job, I can perform really well in that moment.**

- **When I perform well moment after moment after moment, I build up a bank of evidence that tells me I'm good. This gives me confidence.**

- **When I am confident doing something, I want to go and do it again. This fuels my motivation.**

This is simple stuff. If you want to check out the research behind it, feel free to read *Peak Performance Every Time*. However, I suspect you'll see these simple principles reflected in your own life experience.

Should — Need — Want

I often reflect on three levels of motivation that I see. The first is 'should.' I'm sure you've heard people say (or have even said to yourself), "I really should do X." Unfortunately, 'should' is a really weak motivator. Realistically, the chance of us doing something that we 'should' do is pretty small. The things that fall into the 'should' category are typically the things we don't like doing and don't desperately need to do right now. So, they tend to drift so far down the to-do list that they drop off the end and never get done.

'Need' is a much stronger motivator. We often do the things we need to do, even if we don't like them. Interestingly, some tasks that have resided in 'should' territory can get flung into 'need'. I've often reflected that things shift from 'should' into 'need' when we add importance and urgency. I've also noticed that importance and urgency often come with an external push. For example, there's a deadline or a consequence if we don't do it.

Whilst 'need' is a strong motivator, it's also brittle. It's not particularly stable or enduring because it's driven by external circumstances. We wait for the importance and urgency (the deadline, consequence, etc.) to be imposed. And, once those things are no longer present, we'll drift back into 'should' territory again. Managers often tell me that they need to keep on top of people to ensure the work gets done. They use targets, timeframes, and consequences as the motivational stick. They keep looking over people's shoulders to let them know they're being watched. The problem is... what do people do when they're not being watched? What happens if we don't keep imposing new targets, deadlines, and consequences? Or, what happens when the impact of those approaches wears off?

The strongest, most stable, and enduring motivator is 'want'. I often illustrate this through a simple example. Imagine you're at the restaurant and you're looking at the dessert menu. For months, you've been telling yourself to eat healthily, lose some weight, and get fit. Like many people, you want the outcome, but you don't like the process. And, as you look through the dessert menu you see two choices. There's fruit salad. And there's triple chocolate fudge cake with rich chocolate sauce. You think, "I should choose the fruit salad... but I want the chocolate cake." Which dessert are you likely to choose? In a tug of war between 'should' and 'want', 'should' will get its butt kicked every time.

Interestingly, if we change the dynamic slightly, we may get a different outcome. What if you're reading the dessert menu, but this time you've just been diagnosed with something nasty (cancer, or diabetes) and you are now aware just how important healthy choices are. This dynamic may shift you from 'should' into 'need'. You might now think, "I need to choose the fruit salad." But it still doesn't get us into 'want'.

So, how do we get into 'want' territory?

Let's go back to the tasks that we keep putting off because we don't really like them.

I'll often ask people, "Why do you want to do some things and not others?"

The most common answer is, "The things I want to do are the things I enjoy."

It's not rocket science is it?

The question next is, "Why do you enjoy those things?"

When we start following that train of thought, we often come to another simple, but profound understanding. We often enjoy doing things we feel we're good at. Our sense of mastery and enjoyment tend to go hand in hand.

It's probably worth taking a moment to reflect on how this works in your own life.

What do you enjoy doing?

What do you tend to avoid?

Is there a link between those things you feel good at, and the things you enjoy?

Do you tend to avoid the 'harder' things, which take more effort and give you less sense of achievement?

The power of asking these questions is that it often helps us plot the path from 'should' to 'want'. If we want to create more enjoyment, we often need to create a greater sense of achievement. To do this, it makes sense to practice, develop our skills, recognise our progress, and celebrate the improvement we're making. This fuels our sense of achievement and can really drive motivation.

Accomplishment, Ambition and Excellence

I've encountered a lot of high achievers that, by their own admission, are not particularly passionate about what they do. But they are passionate about winning. They get a real buzz from hitting the goal or exceeding the target. They want to be the best.

I know this example is a little stereotypical (possibly even a cliché), but I've often seen this tendency in sales executives. I've encountered a lot who genuinely don't care what they're selling. They are not motivated by the product they sell. Many aren't even particularly interested about what the product does or how it impacts people. The bit that really motivates them is 'the thrill of the chase', as some of them describe it, and the buzz they get from closing a deal.

Of course, this is not just true for sales executives. I've also encountered a lot of athletes who have lost their love for their sport but are still motivated by their hunger for success. Equally, I've met lots of business founders who do have a sense of purpose and want to make money. But their biggest driver is their desire to be number one in their industry, to stand head and shoulders above their competition and be regarded as 'the best.' This ambition often drives people to excel.

Many people find a slight variation to this. They are motivated to be part of an organisation that is regarded as 'the best.' I suspect it's the reason that many people support the best sports teams or want to be associated with leading brands. It's the reason many people buy and wear sports merchandise. Equally, it's the reason why many world-class organisations have a queue outside the door whenever they're recruiting. When I wrote *Hire Great People*, I reflected on the reason why soldiers want to join the Special Forces, Royal Air Force pilots want to join the Red Arrows and athletes want to represent their country. Simply put, people want to join them because they are the best. Getting selected to work with an organisation which is amongst the very best in the world, often provides a huge sense of achievement.

The power of progress

Attainment and accomplishment are not the only motivators though. The recognition that we're improving and progressing also motivates people. I've started learning to fly. So far, it's taken me almost two years to get approximately halfway through my training. It could easily take another two years to complete it and receive my Private Pilot's License. Last week, my brother shared a newspaper article featuring a 17-year-old girl who had completed her training and earned her license within seven weeks. On one hand, I could get disheartened that the training is taking so long, and I haven't yet achieved the goal. I've been waiting to do my first solo flight for over a year. However, I'm enjoying the journey. I can see my progress. More importantly, I recognise and appreciate the progress I've made. I can do things now, like landing and taking off, that seemed unimaginable when I first sat in the left-hand seat of an aeroplane. This sense of progress provides real motivational fuel.

But...

Whilst purpose, enjoyment and a sense of achievement are all very powerful motivators, most people require another dimension as well.

Most people need and want to get paid.

CHAPTER 4

R is for Reward (and Recognition)

Importantly, the 'R' in P.E.A.R. stands for Reward and Recognition.

The brass tacks

When I ask most employees why they come to work, the headline answer is, "To get paid." This answer is often followed by, "There are bills to pay and kids to feed."

Of course, that's the cold hard reality for most people. However, as we discovered in the introduction, that doesn't answer the question, "Why do you come here and do this stuff, with us?" The answer to that question may not be, "Because it's the best paid job."

Let's be honest, there are some professions that people probably wouldn't do if it was purely about the money. Nowadays I suspect that nursing, teaching, care work and many other occupations fall into that category. Whilst people obviously need to get paid, money clearly isn't their biggest motivator. People don't choose careers in nursing to become insanely wealthy or live a billionaire lifestyle. However, it doesn't stop people in those professions striking over pay and conditions.

When I dig under the surface, I often find that people simply want to know that they are being paid a fair wage for the job they do. They want to know that their salary reflects the effort they put in and they are recognised for the value they bring. This is as true for a junior nurse working 12-hour shifts for a little over £20,000 per year, as it is for a Premier League footballer earning tens (or even hundreds) of thousands per week. On one level it sounds bizarre that a Premier League footballer might quibble over salary. However, they are not comparing their salary to a doctor, nurse, fire fighter or teacher. They are comparing their pay to those around them. When I hear players complaining about pay, it's normally because there's another player in the team who is contributing less but being paid more. On that basis, their salary seems unfair. That's no different to conversations you'd hear on a building site, the staff room in a school, or on a nursing ward. The number of zeros on their pay slip may change, but the core issues are the same.

People want to feel like they are rewarded fairly.

Bonuses, commissions, and incentives

When I ask most employers what they think the 'Reward' element in P.E.A.R.-shaped motivation refers to, they talk about bonuses, commissions, and incentives. Surely these rewards motivate most people... right?

Experience tells me that the answer is, "Yes... and No."

Yes, bonuses, commissions and incentives can be motivational. However, many companies have generous bonus schemes and commission structures, but are still struggling to motivate their people. In some cases, the 'bonus' loses its power because people start to expect it. I know businesses who provide a very generous annual bonus every year (normally just before Christmas). Because they provide it every year, the workforce starts to think of it as a lump-sum salary payment. They forget that it's a bonus and begin to expect it. In fact, when one business announced that there would be no bonus, because the company hadn't hit its profit targets, there was almost a mutiny. Arguably the 'bonus' had a negative impact on motivation.

Elite sports players and athletes often have win bonuses. Interestingly, in many cases the win bonus is so small, as a percentage of their mega salary, it makes almost no impact. I remember talking to a coach in Premier League club about this issue. He reflected that during his playing days, the win bonus was equivalent to a week's salary. When he played, his basic wage was enough to live on, but not enough to buy luxuries or go on fancy holidays. However, if they added a win bonus each week, they could afford the nicer things in life. Therefore, the win bonus became a genuine incentive.

I've also seen the motivational power of commissions dry up in sales environments. Over the years I've heard many sales managers talking to their people about commissions. Typically, they will ask, "What will you do with the money?". I remember a recruitment leader asking this question to one of their new consultants. This was the consultant's first job after leaving university. They were desperate to earn some decent money, live life, go out, buy a car, go on holiday, and buy themselves some nice things. So, to begin with, they had a little shopping list in their head. However, over time, the consultant ticked off more and more things from the list. They bought themselves a car and a nice watch. They took themselves out for dinner and went on a few holidays. And, unsurprisingly, their hunger for the commission cheque started to wane. Perhaps it's also not a massive surprise that their appetite for commission resurfaces when they're looking to raise a deposit for their first home... or they learn that their first child is on the way. It reminds us that the commission in itself is not necessarily motivating. The meaning it has for the individual is key.

Over the years, I've learned that many people are aware of the trade-off between earning more money and committing more time and energy into their work. Put simply, there is a cost to earning the bonus. I've noticed that Covid gave people a new perspective on this. They began to question whether the time was more valuable to them than the money. Some concluded that they'd rather have the time.

The point is... bonuses, commissions and incentives are great as long as we understand the context and why people will be driven by them. Some people are money-oriented. Some are materialistic. Those people are likely to be consistently motivated by the prospect of earning more. However, not everyone is wired that way. Most people are motivated by bonuses when they have a specific need or desire. It highlights that money isn't always the greatest incentive. Bizarrely, I've seen 'team pizzas', or a team night out, have a greater motivational impact than cash incentives on occasions.

The power of recognition

When I wrote *Stronger Together*, and studied world-class teams, I began to appreciate the profound difference between two words that sound similar. There's a significant difference between feeling 'valued' and 'valuable'.

Very simply, we feel valued when someone says, "Thank you. Great job."

However, we feel valuable when we realise the difference we make, the impact we have and why our contribution matters. This often happens when leaders say go slightly beyond saying, "Thank you," and say, "Thank you for..."

I remember reflecting on the power of this a few years ago. My 40th birthday present from my wife and daughters, was a trip to Edinburgh for the weekend. We arrived at our hotel early, so the room wasn't quite ready. The member of staff who met us, asked if we'd like a drink whilst they finished preparing the room. I ordered green tea. Caroline asked for peppermint. Once we'd finished our tea, he told us that the rooms were ready and gave us our keys. As he did so, he said, "I notice that neither of you drink English breakfast tea. The tea bags in your room are English breakfast tea, so I thought you might like these." And he handed us a selection of herbal tea bags. It was one of those little personal touches that make a difference and create a great customer experience.

So, once we'd settled into our room, we emailed the hotel chain (which was a national chain with hundreds of outlets across the country) with some glowing feedback. The reply we got back tells us how much importance they place on recognising their people. The message read, "Thank you, we'll let Stephen know."

I wonder how many organisations take the time to ensure the positive customer feedback gets to the people who need to hear it. How often does this feedback reach the customer service team, but go no further? In some cases, I suspect the organisation builds it into a generalised message with customer feedback that might go out to the whole company. But how often do they let those people who create a positive experience know that what they've done has been appreciated? And, if they did, what impact could that have on the motivation of their people?

If Stephen learns that we really appreciated the tea bags, how likely is he to go out of his way to help another customer?

This helps us realise that recognition can come in all kinds of forms, from a few words of thanks to formal recognition. In some cases, the formal version may come as an award. It could be an individual award, such as 'employee of the month.' Equally, it could be a collective award that is presented to a team or the whole organisation. However it comes, there's no doubt that recognition can be incredibly motivating.

Of course...

There's no doubting that people's motivation is likely to be eroded if they don't feel like they're fairly rewarded for the value and effort they give. There's also no doubt that bonuses, commissions, and incentives can be highly motivating. However, many organisations mistakenly think that simply paying people and creating a bonus structure will be enough to motivate their people. In my experience, that's flawed thinking. In reality, there's far more to it than that.

CHAPTER 4.5

Interdependence and overlaps

There's a temptation, when seeing motivation through the lens of the four elements of Purpose, Enjoyment, Achievement and Reward, that we start to view them as independent or separate.

Interdependence

The truth is, they're far from independent. In fact, they're interdependent. They feed one another. I've experienced a simple example in my own life. I know that when I'm passionate about something and feel a sense of purpose, I'm more likely to follow that passion. When I do that, I'll tend to dedicate myself to it. I'll learn more, build up my expertise and develop my skills. As a result, I'll probably gain a greater sense of both enjoyment and achievement. And, if I'm good at what I do, I'll probably also receive more recognition and reward. No doubt, you'll have found something similar.

The inter-dependence means that one of these drivers can feed the others. As we start to develop one, there can often be a positive knock-on impact on the others. It's also true that a decline in one can lead to a decline in others.

Overlaps

There are also many overlaps between these four motivational drivers. There are no absolute divides between these elements. In truth, they emerged because I was trying to make sense of the array of different answers I'd had to the question, "Why do you come here and do this stuff with us?" In particular, there are overlaps between 'Purpose' and 'Enjoyment'. It's hard to know whether 'being passionate' about something lives within 'Purpose' or 'Enjoyment'. Arguably, it's a part of both. Equally, there are obvious overlaps between 'Enjoyment' and 'Achievement'. The understanding that we tend to enjoy those things we feel we're good at emphasises this.

There are drivers that other authors emphasise, such as having a feeling of autonomy and empowerment, that cross several elements too. Having autonomy and being given the freedom to make decisions can make work more challenging and stimulating, so provide a greater sense of enjoyment. It also enables some people to feel recognised and valued. When we take on more responsibility and do a good job, it also provides a sense of achievement. For some, the increased status provides the biggest motivational kick.

So, it stands to reason that there are drivers, such as autonomy, that can tick several boxes. Interestingly, when we begin to understand the individual motivational make-up of people, we can start to see which aspects of autonomy drive each person. Is it status or recognition? Is it challenge? Is it the sense of achievement?

No doubt, giving people autonomy can be incredibly motivating for some people. It could be seen as a broad-brush solution, because it has the potential to tick a lot of boxes. However, I'd argue that understanding their individual motivational profile helps us to know the person and what really makes them tick.

CHAPTER 5

What makes us tick?

What makes you tick?

What makes your people tick?

Why does it help to know?

The truth is...

Motivation is easy when things are going well.

But what happens when they're not?

What happens if things get tough?

I'm pretty sure everyone has experienced situations where their motivation starts to ebb away. I suspect you've seen other people's motivation fluctuate too. Often, we can tie this back to a change in circumstance. But we may not realise why that change has such as profound impact on our motivation.

For example...

Sales executives who are driven primarily by rewards will often find it difficult to motivate themselves in a tough market where sales are hard to come by and bonuses dry up.

Those who are motivated by achievement will become disengaged if they feel like they, and their organisation, are going backwards.

People who love working in a great team and a great environment will become demotivated if the culture goes south.

And we'll tend to lose those who are purpose-driven if our organisation becomes ruthlessly focused on 'the bottom line'.

So, understanding what makes us tick, enables us to motivate ourselves and those around us. The challenge, of course, is that everyone is wired differently. Therefore, we need a way to find out what motivates each individual.

Our motivational profile

Experience tells me that we all have a personal motivational profile, which helps us to know what really drives us. Like personality profiles, I've come to learn that we are all driven by all four elements. But the motivational power and impact that each of these four has, changes from person to person. Here are a few examples, to show how it works.

These are some of the employees at Widget Ltd, a small manufacturing and engineering business that employs around 100 people.

––––––––––––

Chris is an engineer who left his corporate job and founded Widgets Ltd. When Chris reads the four elements of P.E.A.R., he recognises all of them in himself. He regards himself as purpose-driven, having invented the 'widget' because he saw an opportunity to help people. He enjoys many elements of his job, particularly getting involved in solving some of the tougher technical engineering challenges. He also has a strong desire to build a company that is regarded as the leader in its field. And, although he doesn't often talk about it, he likes earning good money and wants to provide a wonderful lifestyle for his family.

Jo is a Sales Director. She has been in sales roles since leaving university and loves it. She hasn't always loved the products she's sold — such as petrochemicals or telecommunications – but she revels in the cut and thrust of sales and doing deals with customers. Jo has been at Widgets Ltd for a year now. She was attracted to the job, partly because it offered her a chance to become a director and partly because she's always wanted to sell something that makes a difference to people. Whilst she likes the seniority and the more strategic elements of her job (plus the salary and benefits), she often misses being at the coal face.

Andy is a highly respected and sought-after software developer, who joined Widgets Ltd a little over two years ago. Within weeks of joining Widgets Ltd, he received multiple offers from multinational corporations, offering roles with higher salaries and better perks. Despite a steady flow of similar offers during the last few years, Andy chooses to stay. When his friends ask why he's still at Widgets, he says, "I like the people. The work is interesting. It pays okay, and I don't need much money."

Marie is the Finance Director at Widgets Ltd. She worked as the company's accountant before joining full-time, so has been with the business from the start. Over the years, she's seen her role grow from purely dealing with accounts and finance, to now overseeing the IT function, looking after the facilities and even HR. Marie works long hours. If she's honest, she would probably rather not have the extra responsibilities, but she knows it's needed in a business of their size. She feels a huge sense of loyalty to Chris, the team, and the company, and takes great pride in doing a good job.

These examples show that each of these people has a blend of the P.E.A.R. elements. However, the proportions of each element change. Most people have a dominant element, a secondary, tertiary, and least dominant driver. When we understand these, a profile emerges.

Ten blocks

Here's a really simple way of assessing our motivational drivers. You can use this little exercise with yourself and others.

You have ten blocks.

Use these ten blocks to best reflect your motivational drivers.

As long as you assign at least **one block to each element**, you can put the other six wherever you like.

Ten blocks example

From this example we can see this individual is highly motivated by reward or recognition, closely followed by enjoyment and then achievement and ambition; making purpose the lowest of their motivational drivers.

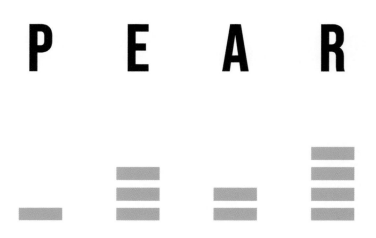

Your ten blocks

Now give it a try for yourself.

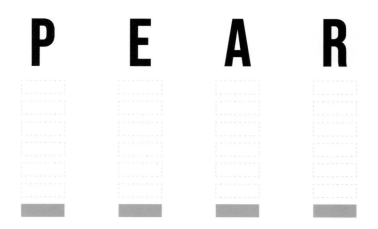

Now that you've assigned your ten blocks, what does it tell you about your motivation?

Now, think about your people.

How might theirs look?

If you know people pretty well, you might be able to make an educated guess about their profile. Equally, you could share the 'ten blocks' exercise with them and get their perspective.

I've found this process to be incredibly insightful, especially if we use it as a way to open up a conversation about what really motivates and drives us. Honestly, whilst the exercise is enlightening, the real value comes from the conversation that follows.

Your people's ten blocks

P   E   A   R

Now that you've assigned your people's ten blocks, what did they tell you about their motivational drivers?

CHAPTER 5.5

One-dimensional motivation

What happens if we have one very dominant motivational driver, and three that are weaker?

Experience tells me that whilst motivation can be strong with only one driver, it is also vulnerable.

Image a sales executive or recruitment consultant who is heavily motivated by rewards. They are almost exclusively driven by the prospect of bonuses and commissions. Someone who is 'R' oriented will be fine whilst they are hungry for the rewards and they're getting their commissions. But what happens if the economic conditions change? What happens when the sales and commission cheques start to dry up?

The likelihood is that if the rewards are no longer there, this person's motivation will evaporate pretty quickly.

Of course, it's not just true for someone that is heavily driven by rewards. The same would be true for someone who is purpose-driven, who finds themselves in an increasingly ruthless, profit-focused, environment. I've seen organisations and managers change from embracing their purpose, to becoming fixated on their bottom line when they feel under pressure. If that happens, those who are heavily purpose-driven are likely to become disengaged.

Those who are largely driven by enjoyment would find their motivation waning if the team dynamic deteriorated, the challenge or stimulation of their role diminished, or the environment started to become overly serious. I've been working with the Fiji Rugby 7s team recently. They are an elite team. The expectation to win gold is massive. It would be very easy to focus everything on winning. However, fun is an enormously important element within their environment and culture. If that starts to dry up, the players will disengage quickly, and the results will follow. As a side note... I'd argue that this isn't just true for the Fiji Rugby 7s team. It's true in many organisations. Interestingly, I've seen hundreds of KPIs that measure profit but very few related to enjoyment.

And those who are predominantly driven by the desire to achieve will find that their motivation nose-dives if they lose the sense that they and the organisation are at the top of their game. Interestingly, I've seen elite athletes who became disillusioned when the team took its foot off the gas and the standards dropped. I also noticed that applications to join the Royal Air Force aerobatic display team — The Red Arrows — reduced when they received negative coverage in the media.

The simple message here is that if we (or our people) are largely driven by one element and it starts to dry up, our motivation is likely to follow. Therefore, it makes sense to build four strong pillars of motivation. Having four strong pillars makes our individual motivation more stable and enduring. It allows us to weather more storms.

It also helps us to create a stronger motivational environment within our teams.

CHAPTER 6

The extra dimension

"If everyone is motivated differently, how am I supposed to motivate my team?"

Understanding a person's motivational profile can help us identify their drivers and therefore motivate them. But how does that help motivate a team, or even and organisation, with vastly different people?

The answer is simple.

We create four strong pillars of motivation within the organisation. We build a motivational environment that has something for everyone.

Imagine for a moment that we had all four elements of P.E.A.R. in abundance.

Imagine we...

Had a strong sense of purpose... we knew that what we did was important, it had a positive impact on the world and made a difference.

A sense of achievement... we knew we were really good at what we did (we might even be the best in our field), we were always improving, growing and developing.

Had a great team, worked with great customers and enjoyed the challenges we took on.

Were recognised and rewarded for the effort we put in and the contribution we made.

If we had these four critical components... what else do we need?

As well as catering for all motivational profiles and ticking everyone's box, when we have four strong pillars, we also create a magical extra dimension.

We have a place that people are proud to belong to.

Feeling proud to belong somewhere is like motivational rocket fuel.

Not only does it inspire people to go the extra mile and give more. It also creates magnetism when recruiting and 'stickiness' that boosts retention.

Proud to belong

The need to belong is deeply ingrained in us, as a species. In fact, Roy Baumeister, one of the world's foremost researchers on belonging, describes it as "a fundamental human need" that stems from our ancestral roots (Baumeister & Leary, 1995). Psychological research shows that belonging is central to happiness, mental health and wellbeing, resilience, engagement, and performance in a vast array of different settings including education and business (Allen, et al, 2021). The research also highlights that our need to belong extends beyond the need to feel socially connected and avoid loneliness. Belonging also means feeling accepted, feeling like we matter and that we're important (Carr, 2019), which has a huge impact on our self-esteem (Baumeister & Leary, 1995).

Evan Carr's article in the Harvard Business Review (Carr, et al, 2019) reveals the impact that this has on workplaces. They report that 'high belonging' is linked to a 56% increase in job performance. They also noted a 50% drop in employee turnover, a 75% reduction in sick days taken, and that employees with a high sense of belonging were 18 times more likely to get promoted. Higher workplace belonging has also been linked with a 167% increase in employer promoter scores (i.e., employees recommend their company to their friends), which has a positive impact on recruitment. All of this suggests that creating an organisation where people feel a sense of belonging pays dividends. However, their research also suggests that over 40% of people report feeling isolated in their work.

But belonging is only one piece of this jigsaw. Being proud to belong also requires a feeling of pride. This could come from the belief that the work we do is important and makes a difference. It could come from the understanding that we're really good at what we do (we might even be the best). This could be driven by our results. Equally, it might emanate from the understanding that our standards and quality are sky-high. Or it could come from how we do it — e.g., we work ethically and with moral integrity. Researchers from Oxford University showed that police officers in Africa felt a greater sense of pride in their work when they knew it was underpinned by values and ethical practice (Harris, et al, 2022).

Life experience tells us that human beings often like to align themselves with success. It's the reason that many sports fans follow winning teams. Not only do we have a desire to belong. We also like to belong to something we feel proud about. Daniel Wann (2006), a professor of psychology at Murray University, describes how our psychological connection with an organisation comes when we feel emotionally invested in its success and failure. Edward Hirt, a professor of psychological and brain science at Indiana University, goes on to explain that a sports fan's connection with their team becomes highly personal. In his words, "It becomes part of their identity." Sports fans see 'fanship' of their team as being part of who they are. This of course, means that their sense of belonging also comes with huge loyalty (Hirt, et al, 1992).

Edward Hirt goes on to say, "The most powerful thing we found was that for highly allied fans, they really did view the team's success akin to how they would view personal success" and that "the team is an extension of the self."

Jonathan Jenson, a professor of sport administration from the University of North Carolina describes how people engage in...

'BIRGing' — Basking In Reflected Glory

and

'CORFing' — Cutting Off Reflected Failure (Sima, 2023).

It probably explains Andrew Billings' findings. He studied over 7000 social media posts from sports fans discussing their teams' results. When their teams won, fans tend to use words like "we", "us" and "our". When their teams lose, fans tend to switch to "they", "them" and "their" (Sima, 2023).

The same principles apply to people working for organisations. The sense of personal connection, emotional investment and 'reflected glory' all impact on whether we feel proud to belong to an organisation. And, like sports fans, it can lead to a deep sense of loyalty.

Of course, winning and success are obvious sources of pride. But they are not the only sources. There are many thousands of sports fans around the world who don't follow winning teams. Yet they remain loyal, nonetheless. In many cases they will follow their home-town team, regardless of their results — that's a curse I know well. In some cases, they follow their team because of what they stand for.

It's more than just winning

One of the best examples I've seen of this is a German football club called FC St. Pauli, who play in Hamburg. FC St. Pauli is the smaller of the two professional teams in Hamburg. Typically, they find themselves in the second tier of German football, although they occasionally make a fleeting appearance in the top tier. On the surface, there is nothing particularly special about this club. They don't win many trophies or have world superstars in their ranks. And, yet they have a global following with supporters' clubs around the world.

Their stadium holds 29,200 people. Every week — win, lose or draw — they have 29,200 in the stands. In fact, they have a 20-year waiting list for season tickets and their merchandise can be seen all over the world.

Why?

Because people want to be associated with them, not for success or winning, but for what they stand for.

FC St. Pauli are very openly anti-racist, anti-discrimination, and anti-fascism. They are openly inclusive and tolerant, with Pride flags often seen flying above the stadium. The club embraces social responsibility and does a huge amount of work in the community to support underprivileged local people. They even started manufacturing their own shirts and merchandise to ensure that they aren't produced by sweat shops. So, their fans care less about their win/loss record, or where they sit in the league table, and more about their values (Hesse, 2015).

The bottom line...

All of this shows that our desire to belong to an organisation we feel proud of is a HUGE motivational driver.

The good news is that we can create a place that people are proud to belong to by building four strong pillars.

CHAPTER 7

Four strong pillars

Having four strong pillars gives us the best chance of creating stable and enduring motivation for individuals, an environment that can drive everyone and the magical extra dimension — a place where everyone is proud to belong.

So, the $64 million question is...

How can we build four strong pillars?

There are some principles that can get us started.

Your motivation

How can you start to strengthen your pillars of motivation?

PURPOSE	ACHIEVEMENT	ENJOYMENT	REWARD
Understand the difference I make Find out how my work changes lives Realise the value and impact I have	Make sure all goals and targets MEAN SOMETHING (or bin them) Tap into learning/ improving and realising progress.	If I work on my skills and know I'm getting better. I start to enjoy it more, so I can fall in love with the processes.	Celebrate the wins. Tap into more of the feedback from clients, colleagues, etc. Drive my performance results and £££

The principles are a great start. But how do we put them into practice in our own environment?

Here are a few ideas and examples that I've encountered on my travels, which might spark your thinking.

Purpose

Some organisations have a compelling purpose. In some cases, they save lives, protect people, or give people better lives. However, not all organisations have an obvious 'grand purpose'. This is a challenge I've been thrown by leaders on a regular basis.

So, what if your organisation isn't in the business of saving lives?

Here are a couple of examples from my work.

A Michelin-starred restaurant.

A friend of mine — Kenny — is a Michelin-starred chef. To produce truly great food and an amazing experience, he needs his people to care deeply about what they do and how they do it. Their standards are sky-high and constantly rising. Quality is critical. The work is challenging and demanding. The hours are unsociable. Therefore, to achieve the level of excellence they require every single day, he needs a team who are completely dedicated.

So, what's their purpose?

He is well aware that eating gourmet food is not essential to human life. Whilst humans need food and drink to survive, they don't need Michelin-starred food. So, what's the purpose of a Michelin-starred restaurant? What gives his people a sense of purpose and an understanding that what they do matters?

Kenny knows that, for many of his customers, eating in a Michelin-starred restaurant could be a once in a lifetime experience. For the majority, it will be something they do on a very special birthday (often one that ends on a zero) or a milestone wedding anniversary. Therefore, he wants their experience to be incredible. He wants to create a memory that they will cherish for many years... even decades.

To do this, he invests heavily in his people, their passion, and their sense of purpose. He'll set his alarm early and take chefs out to forage for ingredients. He'll take them to meet the farmers who rear lambs or grow heritage carrots. This helps the chefs to realise how much care and work goes into putting the ingredients on their work bench. As Kenny knows, respecting the ingredients is a key part of creating exceptional food.

Of course, this thinking doesn't just apply to chefs. He also invests into his sommeliers and waiting staff. He'll often give his front-of-house team the customer experience, so that they understand the importance of getting the little things right. All of this reinforces their connection with the purpose and an understanding of how they contribute to it.

I shared this example with the owner of an architects' practice in London a few years ago. His immediate response was, "Yeah, I see how that works in a Michelin-starred restaurant, but what about an architects' practice?" He explained that architecture can become very functional and transactional (like many jobs). The vast majority of projects aren't related to award-winning or iconic buildings such as The Shard. Most jobs are less much prestigious. The day-to-day reality often revolves around building regulations, planning applications, difficult clients, etc. It's easy to get so caught up in the daily grind that we lose sight of the purpose.

So, we started discussing it.

I asked him, "What impact do truly great buildings have on people? For example, how would a great office space improve people's working lives, or their experience whilst at work? Would it make their life easier on a practical level? How would it impact on someone's thinking, mood, or emotions?".

Interestingly, as I asked the question his demeanour changed. He lit up. He became animated and started telling me all about some of the great buildings he'd been in, what made them special and the impact they had. Then I asked if he'd ever taken his architects out to some of the great buildings in London to help them reconnect with their passion for architecture and the importance of designing wonderful buildings that make a positive impact on the people who use them.

The truth is, when we look for it, we can often start to reconnect with both passion and purpose. But, to see, we must look.

And, once we've found those things that fuel our passion and purpose, we need to keep focusing on them or they'll drift out of sight.

Enjoyment

Some jobs are fun. Some tasks are enjoyable. But, let's be honest, there aren't too many. Even when people enjoy the core of their role, they may not enjoy the peripheral jobs that need doing. For example, a teacher who loves teaching a class full of students may not enjoy the growing amount of reporting and administration that goes hand-in-hand with the role.

So, if we can't eliminate the boring bits or exclusively work on the fun tasks, how can we build the enjoyment pillar?

When people describe where the enjoyment comes from, most will talk about their team. Fundamentally, they'll talk about being part of a great team and working with other great people. Therefore, it makes sense to recruit great people. When I talk about recruiting great people, I'm not just talking about employees. I'm also talking about suppliers, partners, members, and clients. To do this, we need to know what great people look like and be selective about who we bring into the environment.

In *Hire Great People*, I share the simple (not easy) approach that world-class organisations use to hire on character. If we break this down to its simplest component parts, we need to...

- Become a 'magnet for talent' — a place where great people want to belong.

- Understand the critical characteristics we're looking for in people — the top three or four.

- Know how to test for these characteristics — make people demonstrate them.

- Notice if things aren't working early on and be decisive (because not even the best in the world get it right every time).

Following this simple approach will help us create a positive culture that can fuel everyone's enjoyment.

But having great people around us is not the only element that creates enjoyment. As we discovered in Chapter 3, the balance between the challenge and our skills (or more specifically our perception of the challenge and our belief in our skills) plays a huge part.

If the skills outweigh the challenge, many people get bored. If the challenge exceeds the skills, a lot will get demoralised.

Interestingly, my experiences over the last few decades tell me that both imbalances are often prevalent in the workplace. There are a lot of people who train for a profession, reach a level of competence, and then stagnate. When they stop to think about it, a lot of those will say that when they first started the job, it was exciting. They'll talk fondly about the steep learning curve and challenges in the early years of their role. Many will also reflect on how that dynamic has changed in recent times and how their focus has switched to ticking off their never-ending to-do list.

Equally, many people find that they procrastinate over things they're not confident in. They shy away from things that are outside their comfort zone because they require a lot more effort. Of course, if we don't feel like we're very good at something, the chances are we won't feel the sense of satisfaction from doing it well either.

The story behind the story.

A while ago I embarked on a mission, to write my first fictional book. I'll be honest, when I set out, I expected it to be pretty straightforward. Having written eight non-fiction books, I thought, "How different can this be?" I quickly learned that it's very different. In fact, in many cases, it's the polar opposite. Non-fiction writing is based on 'telling'. Writing fiction requires the author to 'show not tell'. And it quickly became apparent that I'd need to unlearn much of what I'd learned about writing.

The first real test came when I sent my second draft to an editor for feedback.

I'd been working hard on it for a year or so. The manuscript was 83,000 words. I thought it was pretty good, so sent it off expecting to hear largely positive feedback with a couple of things to work on. A few weeks later I received an email from the editor. The subject line read, "Book feedback (brace yourself)." His opening line was, "The good news is that, technically, you have a story because it has a start, middle and end. But that's where the good news finishes." And then he fired both barrels. "If I was being uber-generous, I'd say the manuscript was a 2/10. Realistically, it was probably more like a 1/10."

Here's my problem.

At that point, I found the process of writing fiction really tough. It wasn't natural. The words didn't flow. Whenever I sat down to write, it felt like I was wading through treacle. It was not enjoyable. And I was clearly terrible. I didn't get a warm fuzzy feeling when I read it back. I had no sense that I was creating something good.

In the early stages, I drew on my sense of purpose — the reason I started writing the book in the first place. My reason was to help people (particularly teenagers) to navigate their own mental and emotional challenges. It was a compelling reason to start and therefore a reason to keep going, no matter how hard I was finding it. It was this sense of purpose that spurred me on to keep learning, improving, and developing my fiction writing.

Gradually, the 1/10 draft improved. By the time I'd done the fifth draft, it was around a 5/10 (maybe a 6/10). After another couple of drafts, it was a 7/10. And eventually, by the twelfth full draft, it was good enough to publish.

Interestingly, as my skills improved, so did my enjoyment. By the end of the process, I looked forward to sitting down at the computer and writing. I'd also read little pieces back to myself and think, "That bit is not bad" or (very occasionally), "That bit might be quite good."

If you fancy seeing the end product, visit silenceyourdemons.co.uk.

The experience highlights the need to create the balance between challenge and skills. Sometimes this comes when we adjust the challenge. Often it comes when we develop our skills and confidence.

If you can see someone who is struggling it's often wise to see how you can simplify things, build their skills (and confidence), and then watch the motivation rekindle.

Achievement and Ambition

The selection process for the UK Special Forces is notoriously brutal, in some cases fatal.

So, why do hundreds of soldiers apply for a handful of places every single year?

Just 15% of those applying for Oxford or Cambridge University will get an offer. The application process is far more demanding that most universities.

So, why do thousands of students apply to Oxbridge every year?

The simple answer to both questions is, "They're the best."

Being part of an organisation that is regarded as 'the best' is hugely motivating for some. It engenders a massive feeling of pride in many people and is an obvious way of strengthening the achievement and ambition pillar.

The question is...

What if we're not our industry's equivalent of the Special Forces or Oxbridge?

—————

In truth, most organisations don't start out as the best in their field. Only a rare few will ever stand out and be recognised as 'the best'. However, I'd argue that we all have the opportunity to be on the journey. We can focus on ramping up the standards and quality of what we do and recognise the improvements and progress along the way. This shows that we're on the path to excellence before we reach the pinnacle.

—————

My lesson from the Olympic programmes.

In 2004, I began working with an organisation called the English Institute of Sport. Our job was to provide sport-science support to the Team GB Olympic programmes and England teams. When we set out, there were some well-established programmes, such as the US Olympic Committee and Australian Institute of Sport. During the first couple of years, we looked up to them and aspired to reach their level. We worked diligently to drive our standards upwards and emulate their programmes.

In around 2006 we became aware that the quality of our work matched, and in many cases surpassed, both the US and Australian programmes. This realisation had a profound impact. Whenever I pulled on my black polo shirt and tracksuit, I felt a little tingle of pride. We were setting the pace in many ways. We'd become the programme to follow.

Interestingly, at that time, we didn't have the medals to prove it. We won a few at the Commonwealth Games in 2006, but the real confirmation didn't come until the Beijing Olympics in 2008, which was reinforced in London in 2012.

As I reflected on this, the initial injection of pride came from the standard of our processes and the quality of our work, not the results.

The knowledge that we're growing, improving, and progressing is incredibly motivating for many people. We don't necessarily have to 'be the best'.

> **Knowing that we're on the path to excellence is hugely motivating and really strengthens our 'A' pillar.**

Reward and Recognition

"We have a tight budget. We can't just increase salaries or throw money at incentives and bonuses."

Unsurprisingly, I've heard these very valid sentiments from leaders on more than one occasion.

So, how can we strengthen the 'R' pillar without throwing more money at it?

The diagram at the start of this chapter gives some clues. In the 'R' column, you'll see phrases like, 'celebrate the wins' and 'tap into positive feedback'. Often, there are things you can do that cost nothing (or very little) yet have a very real impact. It has become a cliché but recognising how far we've come (not just focusing on what still needs to be done), is a simple first step.

Let's celebrate the good stuff we're currently doing, as well as focus on the improvements we need to make.

Organisations will have received positive feedback from customers, clients, or members. However, that feedback doesn't often get to the people who contributed to the good customer experience. Simply getting the feedback to those who were responsible is hugely motivating for them.

Of course, we can also redesign the way we employ our rewards and incentives, so that they become more motivational for more people.

3D Incentives.

In 2007 I began working with a café/restaurant business. They were a small outfit with big ambitions. They wanted to do things differently (and better) but had a very modest budget.

To be successful, we needed a highly motivated team, delivering 'above and beyond' service every day. Like much of the leisure dining sector, our team were largely made up of low-paid, part-time staff, most of whom were on hourly contracts.

Our first step was to recruit the best people we could and offer them 10% more than our competitors. This gave us the ability to say, "We're going to demand more than everyone else, but we're also willing to pay more," and "If you don't want to deliver our standards, you're free to work somewhere else (but they don't pay as well as we do ☺)".

We also constructed a '3D' incentive package to keep everyone interested.

The 3D model is very simple. Unsurprisingly it has three elements; who is rewarded, how they are rewarded and the time-frame.

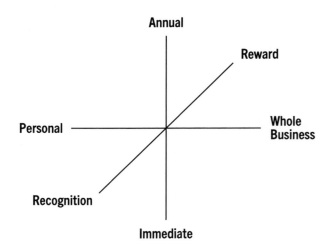

Incentives could be earned by individuals... the team that work together on a particular shift... the team within one café ... or the company as a whole.

We could also reward people for something that happens in the moment (immediate), on that day, during the week, in the month or over the course of a year (annual).

And we could provide a range of rewards from simple recognition (such as saying "well done" or "thank you for...") through prizes and awards, all the way to cash and financial bonuses.

The 3D incentive model was built on creating a variety of incentives across all three dimensions.

For example...

We had a mystery shopper bonus, which was awarded to the team that performed well during a particular shift. If that team hit 8/10 (or more) on each of the mystery shopper criteria scores, every member of the shift team received £50 in cash. It was an 'immediate', 'shift team', 'cash bonus'.

We also had a monthly MVP 'Most Valuable Player' award that went to the individual in each café who was the star team player that month. Their prize had to be personally meaningful. There was a maximum budget of

£50 but the prize had to be worth far more to the recipient than the money. This meant that the leaders needed to know each member of their team and really think about a prize that would be appreciated. It was a 'monthly', 'individual', 'prize'.

Our first winner worked an enormous number of hours in the café. Whenever he wasn't working, he'd be coaching his son to play football. So, for his MVP prize, we created a coaching pack with a football, some cones, football coaching cards and DVDs (that shows you how long ago it was). We also 'borrowed' our Chairman's season tickets so that he could take his son to a Premier League game (which cheated the £50 budget). I bumped into Shayan (who won that prize) years later whilst walking through the city. He told me how he still remembered what we'd done for him and how grateful he was.

As well as these more immediate incentives, we also had wider financial rewards such as the company annual bonus (which was related to the profitability of the whole company).

Interestingly, we found that our thinking around incentives and rewards became far more innovative and had more impact when we used the 3D-model as a guide.

Of course, the most obvious way to increase rewards and recognition is to drive performance and therefore improve results.

CHAPTER 8

Over to you

I end most of my keynote talks and masterclasses with the same message.

If you walk away from this session saying it was "interesting" or "enjoyable", we will have achieved very little. In fact, we'll have missed the biggest opportunity.

The information in this book only becomes valuable when you use it.

So please, take this away, apply it, use it... squeeze every ounce of benefit you can from it.

With that in mind... how are you going to use and apply what you've learned from this book?

How can you now put it into action?

1. How can you build four strong pillars, to create stable and enduring motivation for yourself?

2. How can you build four strong pillars for your team, to motivate those around you?

Your four strong pillars of motivation

PURPOSE	ACHIEVEMENT	ENJOYMENT	REWARD

P   E   A   R

How can you build four strong pillars of motivation for yourself?

Your teams four strong pillars of motivation

PURPOSE	ACHIEVEMENT	ENJOYMENT	REWARD

P E A R

How can you build four strong pillars of motivation for your team?

As with everything, putting these into practice
is the first step. To embed it, you will need to
constantly revisit it, update it, and keep it alive.

Like anything worthwhile, it takes time, plus a little effort and some thought.

But the rewards are incredible.

Thank you for reading *Motivation is P.E.A.R.-Shaped*. I hope you enjoyed it. Please enjoy this introduction to my third book *Two Lengths Of The Pool*.

A WINDOW INTO TWO LENGTHS OF THE POOL

Two Lengths of the Pool... What's it all about?

It seems like a very strange phrase doesn't it. You may well be thinking, "What do the words Two Lengths of the Pool mean, and how on earth does it relate to me and my performance?"

In truth, the Two Lengths of the Pool concept is a very simple idea that I arrived at by accident, whilst working with a Team GB Olympic swimmer called Chris Cook. Although the concept first emerged in a high-performance sporting environment, I've found that, like many other areas of sport psychology, it applies to a wide variety of fields.

For many years, parallels have been drawn between sporting success and success in business. Sports coaches have been employed to help businesses develop a 'winning mentality'. There are numerous books on the market, which also aim to translate successful formulae from the world of sport into the commercial world. The question is, does it really work? Are there lessons that can be taken from sport and applied to business? Could a business that is struggling in the current economic climate actually benefit from the experiences of elite athletes?

In 2010, Chris Cook and I started working with a law firm in the UK, to apply the 'two lengths' concept to their business. They wanted to adopt the very strategies that helped Chris to win medals and break records. In 2008, the commercial climate in the UK became particularly tough for professional firms such as accountancy and legal firms. Noticeably, some well-established and well-respected firms went out of business. This trend has made some leading firms sit up and take note. They realise that to survive and grow in this climate, they need to become smarter and more effective.

So... What is the 'two lengths' concept and where did it come from?

Let's rewind to the beginning of the story.

In 2001, Chris was a national standard swimmer who had just competed at the World Student Games. He was ranked 32nd and had not yet won a full international cap. Between 2001 and around 2004–2005, we worked in a slight fog. Although Chris was making progress, the plan we were working to was a 'best guess'. It was a little bit reactionary. It almost felt like we were navigating in very poor visibility and reacting as things appeared. At the time Chris was working to a set of goals which included, 'making the GB team', 'securing funding', 'securing sponsorship', 'qualifying for championships' and 'winning key races'.

One afternoon, Chris came into my office for one of our regular one-to-one sport psychology sessions. He was looking particularly flustered. When I asked what was wrong, Chris started to explain that he had a lot on his plate; correspondence with British Swimming regarding his funding, arranging travel to competitions, an awards dinner, training, etc. There is a technical term for this condition in sport psychology. Chris was 'a stress head'. After he'd finished, I said,

"That's strange. Surely your job is simply to swim two lengths of the pool as fast as you can."

I have to be honest; Chris didn't take too kindly to this at first. He felt as though I'd undermined and belittled his job. Initially, he thought, "my job is a bit more complicated than that, thank you very much." As he drove from my office at the English Institute of Sport back to the swimming pool, Chris paired my name with a number of choice expletives. As he says himself, his ego was hurting, and it took a little while for him to get his head around the whole idea.

To hear him describing the experience in his own words, watch Chris Cook's session (entitled 'Olympic athlete, Chris Cook, On... Two Lengths of the Pool') at https://www.youtube.com/@SimonHartley

Until that point, we had made a fundamental error. We had got Chris's job wrong. His job was not to make the GB team. It wasn't to secure funding or sponsorship. It wasn't to qualify for championships or win races.

He was a 100m swimmer in a 50m pool. His job was very very simple. The job was to swim two lengths of the pool as quickly as he could.

What impact did this have on Chris's performance?

That realisation was like a blinding flash of light. It made an enormous impact on how he worked, his effectiveness and the end results. Immediately he started to identify exactly what he needed to do in order to swim two lengths of the pool as quickly as he could. He pulled together his team of specialists, which included his coach, physiotherapist, performance analyst, nutritionist, physiologist, strength and conditioning coach, performance lifestyle adviser and me. Everyone was challenged to help him swim two lengths of the pool as quickly as he possibly could. His whole outlook changed once he figured out what his real job was.

It became a benchmark and a filter. Before doing anything, Chris would ask "will this help me swim two lengths of the pool quicker?" He challenged his team whenever he walked into a training session by asking, "How will this session help me to swim two lengths of the pool quicker?" As he walked into each and every training session or competition, Chris knew exactly how it was going to contribute to his performance.

If there was a method, strategy, practice, or technique that would make him quicker, he'd consider doing it. If not, it would be rejected. We also started asking whether it was likely to knock a whole second off his time or 0.000001 seconds. Obviously, the things which made a bigger impact had a higher priority. Chris actually identified the five key processes that he required. These were the processes which had the greatest positive impact on his performance. Once he had identified these, he focused his time and energies into delivering these key processes.

We broke all the rules that never existed

Of course, the 'rules' were never rules. They were conventions. Rather than perpetuating the habits that had governed his training programme for the last few years, we questioned it and challenged it. Were all of these sessions actually contributing? Were they helping Chris swim faster? We turned the whole approach on its head and started by looking at how we could make him quicker. Interestingly, Bradley Wiggins (2012) describes going through a similar process with his sport scientist, Tim Kerrison, in his book *My Time*.

We broke down Chris's stroke. We analysed his technique. He started to figure out what the key elements of his performance were and put programmes in place to improve them. He changed his training regime to remove many of the things he had habitually done (because they had always been on the programme) and replaced them with things that would contribute to swimming two lengths quicker than he had before.

We identified that Chris needed to flatten the angle at his hips to reduce his drag in the water. Out went some of the swim sessions and strength sessions that were not really contributing. In came yoga, gymnastics, and specialist physiotherapy work to improve his streamlining. We also found that he needed more strength in the very first part of his arm movement (the phase of his stroke when his arms were stretched out in front of him). To do this he used gymnastics rings and a climbing wall instead of dumb-bells and weights.

We spent two to three years working on a project to help improve his starts by a few tenths of a second, and another to work on his turns. Chris did some of the sessions in a gymnastics hall, diving into a pit full of foam bricks, rather than a pool full of water. We analysed his performances to find the perfect race strategy for him and then put a programme in place to practice this and perfect it. Chris even found a new warm-up for competitions. Rather than ploughing up and down, swimming lengths with the others, Chris would often sit or lie on the bottom of the pool and simply attune himself with the water.

Interestingly, when he looked back, Chris noticed that he had ditched 60 per cent of his training programme. He questioned whether he needed to swim tens of thousands of metres in the pool every week. When we looked at it honestly and objectively, it became obvious that he had adopted his training programme out of habit, not because it was the most effective possible.

This thought process set up our working practice for the last four or five years of his career. It helped Chris to become infinitely more focused, more effective, and more successful. The results were dramatic. Because he could swim two lengths of the pool more quickly, he won more races, became a regular on the British team (and in fact became British and Commonwealth number one for several years), he qualified for major championships, made finals at World Championships, and Olympic Games, and won two gold medals at the Commonwealth Games. The final race of Chris's career was an Olympic final in Beijing 2008, and he ended his career as the seventh fastest 100m breaststroke swimmer in history.

Does this really apply to me?

Many individuals and organisations are now using exactly the same principles to enhance their own effectiveness, including the UK law firm that I mentioned earlier. They have found their own 'two lengths of the pool'. This is not a mission statement or a vision. Instead, it is a statement of their job in the simplest possible terms. It provides them with the clarity and simplicity that gives them complete focus. The senior partners have also agreed upon the most important processes required to achieve their 'two lengths' successfully. As a result, they can cascade this clear focus throughout the business. They can also establish their own filters and benchmark their effectiveness. To ensure that this new way of working starts to live and breathe and become part of the culture, it has also become embedded in the performance management structures. Everyone's job is aligned to the 'two lengths' for the firm and the processes which are required to achieve it. As a result, every member of the team has a clear focus, which is completely aligned to the firm's main job, their equivalent of the 'two lengths'.

Obviously, the process doesn't happen overnight. The project with the law firm spanned nine months and included several reviews along the way.

Results from the early stages of the project show that the effectiveness of the senior management team has increased significantly. The partners realise that, before the project, there was a significant amount of time spent on 'garbage'. The 'garbage' (aka distractions from their core job) was reducing their effectiveness. The Managing Partner of the firm told me that they have binned 60 per cent of what they were doing because it was not contributing to their 'two lengths'.

Hang on... 60 per cent... haven't we heard that somewhere before?

Pressure... What Pressure?

As well as helping to focus Chris's training, we also found that the 'two lengths of the pool' concept helped to reduce his perception of 'pressure' during competition. Here's an excerpt from an article that I wrote, entitled 'Pressure... What Pressure?' The full article, and accompanying webinar, is available at www.be-world-class.com.

Athletes feel 'pressure' when they get the job wrong. Typically, athletes think that their job is to win, to climb up the rankings, to secure prize money or sponsorship. However, none of those things are the job. Normally when we get the job wrong, it is because we're too busy focusing on the outcome. In reality, our job is to deliver the process. By aiming for the result, we set ourselves a job which is outside of our control. The fact that it is outside of our control means that it's uncertain. Winning is never certain. Hitting a target is never certain. There is always an element of uncertainty. This uncertainty is what tends to cause us the angst. How can we be completely confident in our ability to achieve something that has uncertainty? If you're trying to do an 'impossible' job or even a job which you have no control over, you will probably feel under pressure because you will not be 100 per cent sure that you can do the job. The job might seem too big or too daunting. If the athlete believes the job is to win the tournament, they might doubt their ability to do it. Even a confident athlete won't know that they can do that job. There is often a gap between what we believe we can achieve, and what we think we must achieve. That gap manifests as the worry and anxiety we associate with pressure. This is illustrated in the model of the Challenge and Skills Balance (found on page 46 of *Peak Performance Every Time*, published in 2011 by Routledge). If we create an expectation for ourselves (or take on board someone else's expectations), we create a target.

If we are not absolutely sure that we can achieve that target, we might start to have doubts and worries. If we also give that target some meaning, we will magnify our doubts and worries.

As we've said already, we create pressure therefore we can 'de-construct it'. The easiest way is not to create it in the first place. However, if we do feel pressure, we have the ability to dismantle it and start to see the reality rather than the illusion. If you start to perceive pressure, take a few moments to remind yourself why there is no pressure and never was any pressure. Normally this involves a slight reality check and a quick reminder of the job. Once we do that, we are more likely to be able to focus on exactly what we need to do in that moment. In reality the job we need to do will normally be pretty simple and something we're very capable of doing. Rather than trying to 'serve for the match' or 'win Championship point', we'll simply be trying to serve. Instead of trying to win the World Cup, the job is simply to take a penalty kick. Rather than attempting to win the Ryder Cup, the job is simply to execute a three-foot putt.

Chris knew that his only job was to swim two lengths of the pool as fast as he could. This didn't change, regardless of whether he was in a training session or an Olympic final.

Find out more...

If you'd like to learn more, check out *Two Lengths of the Pool*; Sometimes the simplest ideas have the greatest impact and Simon's other books at https://be-world-class.com/books/

Purchase *Two Lengths Of The Pool*

Amazon UK
amazon.co.uk/dp/1484969855

Amazon USA
amazon.com/dp/1484969855

———————

To find out more about my work
and my other books please visit:
be-world-class.com

BIBLIOGRAPHY

Allen, K-A. (2022). The Science Behind Our Need to Belong. *Psychology Today*. 3 February 2022. Online. Available HTTP: <https://www. psychologytoday.com/us/blog/sense-belonging/202202/the-science-behind-our-need-belong> (accessed 12 December 2023).

Allen, K-A., Gray, D.L., Baumeister, R.F. and Leary, M.R. (2021). The need to belong: A deep dive into the origins, implications, and future of a fundamental construct. *Educational Psychology Review*, 34, pp.1133–1156.

Bandura, A. (1997). *Self-Efficacy: The Exercise of Control*. New York: Freeman.

Baumeister, R.F. and Leary, M.R. (1995). The need to belong: Desire for interpersonal attachments as a fundamental human motivation. *Psychological Bulletin* 117(3), pp.497–529.

Berkow, R. (1984) *The Merck Manual of Diagnosis and Therapy*, 15th Edition. New York: Merck Sharp Publishing.

Carr, E.W., Reece, A., Kellerman, G.R. and Robichaux, A. (2019). The value of belonging at work. *Harvard Business Review*. 16 December 2019. Online Available HTTP: <https://hbr.org/2019/12/the-value-of-belonging-at-work> (accessed 12 December 2023)

Csikszentmihalyi, M. (1990). *Flow: The Psychology of Optimal Experience*. New York: Harper and Row.

Csikszentmihalyi, M. (2008) 'Creativity, fulfillment and flow', *Keynote Presentation to TED Conference*. 24 October 2008. Online. Available HTTP: <http://www.youtube.com/watch?v=fXIeFJCqsPs> (accessed 15 December 2010)

Frankl, V.E. (1959). *Man's Search for Meaning*. New York: Touchstone.

Harris, D., Borcan, O., Serra, D., Telli, H., Schettini, B. and Dercon, S. (2022) Proud to belong: The impact of ethics training on police officers. *Oxford University Research Archive*. Online. Available HTTP: <https://ora. ox.ac.uk/objects/uuid:ea7bcad5-af6e-49d1-9a00-ff20f9c57569>

Hartley, S.R. (2012). *How to Shine; Insights into unlocking your potential from proven winners.* Chichester: Capstone.

Hartley, S.R. (2013). *Could I Do That?* Chichester: Capstone.

Hartley, S.R. (2015). *Stronger Together; How great teams work.* London: Piatkus.

Hartley, S.R. (2015). *How to Develop Character.* Leeds: Be World Class.

Hartley, S.R. (2018). *Master Mental Toughness.* Leeds: Be World Class.

Hartley, S.R. (2022a). *Hire Great People.* Leeds: Be World Class.

Hartley, S.R. (2022b). *Peak Performance Every Time* (Second Edition). Oxford: Routledge.

Hayes, A. (2021). 'This is what it takes to join the SAS', *Men's Health.* May 2021 [available online https://www.menshealth.com/uk/fitness/a36379046/sas-training-selection/] (accessed 12 December 2023).

Hesse, U. (2015). St Pauli: the club that stands for all the right things... except winning. *The Guardian.* 6 September 2015. Online Available HTTP: <https://www.washingtonpost.com/wellness/2022/12/15/sports-fans-team-identity/> (accessed 12 December 2023)

Hill, T. (2010). *Making Character First.* Oklahoma City: Character First Publishers.

Hirt, E.R., Zillmann, D., Erickson, G.A., & Kennedy, C. (1992). Costs and benefits of allegiance: Changes in fans' self-ascribed competencies after team victory versus defeat. *Journal of Personality and Social Psychology,* 63, pp.724–738.

Kerr, J. (2013). *Legacy; What the All Blacks Can Teach Us About The Business Of Life.* London: Constable.

Sima, R. (2023) Self-esteem of sports fans is linked to their team, research shows. *Washington Post.* 9 February 2023. Online. Available HTTP: <https://www.washingtonpost.com/wellness/2022/12/15/sports-fans-team-identity/> (accessed 12 December 2023)

Sinek, S. (2009). *Start With Why; How great leaders inspire everyone to take action.* New York: Penguin.

Wann, D.L. (2006). Examining the potential causal relationship between sport team identification and psychological wellbeing. *Journal of Sport Behavior*, 29, pp.79–95.

Wann, D.L., & Grieve, F.G. (2005). Biased Evaluations of In-Group and Out-Group Spectator Behavior at Sporting Events: The Importance of Team Identification and Threats to Social Identity. *Journal of Social Psychology*, 145, pp.531–545.

ABOUT SIMON HARTLEY

Hi, I'm Simon.

I'm passionate about helping individuals, teams, leaders, and organisations unlock their potential and become world-class in their field.

My background is sport psychology. I've spent much of my career working with elite athletes and sports teams, helping them to get their mental game and their mindset right.

But my real passion is working with and studying the very best in the world. I love figuring out what makes them great and then helping others adopt those principles.

Over the years, I've written a few non-fiction books, to share what I've learned about mindset, teams, leadership, and world-class performance. I also wrote a fiction book, called Silence Your Demons, to help people navigate mental and emotional challenges (which you'll find at https://www.silenceyourdemons.co.uk).

I also share these lessons through my coaching, podcasts and speaking work, and through a few digital programmes.

If you fancy finding out more, feel free to check out my other books.

… and visit the Be World Class website for more.

be-world-class.com

OTHER BOOKS BY SIMON HARTLEY

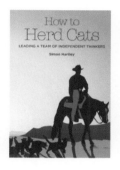

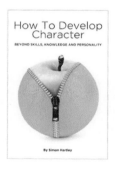